MW00834993

CELEBRATE '98

The Untold Stories Behind the Tennessee Vols' 1998 National Championship

CELEBRATE '98

The Untold Stories Behind the Tennessee Vols' 1998 National Championship

DAVE HOOKER

Fresh Ink Group
Guntersville

Celebrate '98
The Untold Stories Behind
the Tennessee Vols' 1998 National Championship

Copyright © 2023
by Dave Hooker
All rights reserved

Fresh Ink Group
An Imprint of:
The Fresh Ink Group, LLC
1021 Blount Avenue #931
Guntersville, AL 35976
Email: info@FreshInkGroup.com
FreshInkGroup.com

Edition 1.0 2023

Photos courtesy of Stephen Hargis, *Chattanooga Times Free Press*
Photos culled from Facebook & other social media
Photos courtesy of Bill Shipley, shipleyphoto
Photos courtesy of the University of Tennessee
Cover by Stephen Geez / FIG
Book design by Amit Dey / FIG

Except as permitted under the U.S. Copyright Act of 1976 and except for brief quotations in critical reviews or articles, no portion of this book's content may be stored in any medium, transmitted in any form, used in whole or part, or sourced for derivative works such as videos, television, and motion pictures, without prior written permission from the publisher.

Cataloging-in-Publication Recommendations:

SPO083000 SPORTS & RECREATION / College Sports
SPO015000 SPORTS & RECREATION / Football
SPO019000 SPORTS & RECREATION / History

Library of Congress Control Number: 2023915826

ISBN-13: 978-1-958922-46-0 Papercover
ISBN-13: 978-1-958922-47-7 Hardcover
ISBN-13: 978-1-958922-48-4 Ebooks

Dedication

This book is dedicated to two people with incredibly different backgrounds but very similar approaches to life, which is to take true interest in people, care for them and be honest: Glenda Russell, my mother, and Fred White, the former safety and leader who helped guide Tennessee's 1998 football team to a national championship.

Russell, or "Denda" as she is now known by my children, was pretty important in getting to the point in which I could write a book. After all, she gave birth to me. However, she did much more. We'll get to that in a bit. First, let's talk about Fred.

Fred is one of the few people that I've covered in sports that I call a friend. There's always a natural conflict of interests between the media and those they cover in sports. Not with Fred.

This book wouldn't be remotely possible without Fred. His insight into the 1998 team and his willingness to be at the ready to share a phone number, line up an interview or answer a follow-up question is what made this book possible. Without Fred, there is no book. Without Fred, there is no national championship in 1998. Fred helped me assemble this book, but he helped his team even more.

Fred was known as a sort of uncle by his teammates. Fiery linebacker Al Wilson was pretty tough to approach for younger players. Fred wasn't. He was the leader that would put an arm around a freshman like Deon Grant, encourage his former teammates to graduate and, perhaps most importantly, be the person that maintained the bond for a group of men that, like any group of guys, could use a lift now and again. Without Fred, there is no book. And, for the record, he created the term "VFL" even though you probably thought the moniker came from a former Tennessee coach with fancy hair. Fred started the term as a way to keep all former Tennessee football players together.

Now, let's get to Denda.

Denda has taught for 40 years, from elementary school to community college. Yes, she retired, but she kept on teaching developmental reading in college because she loved helping people better themselves. She's done the same with countless family members and friends by tutoring their children for free. Fortunately, she had the same attitude about me.

Denda inspired my genuine interest in people, that everyone has a story and that some need more empathy than others. You never know what someone has been through in life until you actually care enough to ask and listen.

Denda was also challenged with raising a, shall we say, robust teenager that was more than a handful. Patience? Yeah, Denda had enough to fill Neyland Stadium. Denda also instilled a sense that everything doesn't have to work, take chances and realize that life isn't just about a book, a career decision or how much money you make. It's about being a good parent and a good husband. That's a pretty good lesson plan for any teacher.

There have been times in which I have been recognized in public because of media career. Denda is recognized by her thousands of former students who appreciate what she did for their lives, not just their test scores. She's practically an academic celebrity in north Knoxville.

I would also be remiss if I didn't thank my lovely wife, Chanda, who could have done much better. She's been a life partner, the best editor I've ever had and the best counsel you could ever imagine. Perhaps this book would have been possible without Chanda, but it would have had more grammatical errors than a Dr. Seuss book had rhymes.

There have been others along the lines. People that have helped me become a writer, people that have appreciated my work and supported me, but none more important than Denda, Fred and Chanda.

To the three of you, I owe my undying appreciation.

Thank you,
Dave Hooker

Table of Contents

Foreword

While reading Dave Hooker's extraordinary book on the national championship season in 1998, I couldn't help but feel a little sorry for myself. As a proud Tennessee alum, I took pride like everyone else in experiencing every pulsating moment of the season, but it also took me back to my first big game I covered as a student reporter for the *Daily Beacon* in October 1976.

Things were just a little different back then.

Moments after the 20-13 loss to Alabama—the sixth straight loss in the series—I sat on an empty bench in a solemn and spooky locker room with Mickey Marvin, the Vols All-America guard. He attempted to talk once, then twice, but no words came out.

Finally, he lowered his head and tears began rolling down the face of the nearly 300-pound man.

"I can't believe we lost to Alabama," Marvin said slowly. "Now I'll have to tell my grandchildren I never beat Alabama."

I waited patiently and finally left him alone, drowning in his tears and despair. As I looked behind, the sight of him sitting alone was one of the saddest I've ever seen in a lifetime of covering sports. I slowly moved toward the door and outside, a steady rain fell on the quiet turf of Neyland Stadium.

I felt the exact opposite in reliving every wonderful moment in *Celebrate '98: The Untold Stories behind Tennessee Vols' 1998 National Championship*. By 1998, I was long gone from Tennessee, instead parked in Alabama, covering the misbegotten 7-5 Crimson Tide season, which included a 35-18 loss to the Vols. But I took such pride, and yes, held my breath like everyone else, as I feverishly turned the pages in Dave's book—especially the heart-stopping showdown with Arkansas. Reliving that game I literally felt like I was in Neyland that November day.

When I read about the Clint Stoerner fumble, tripping over his lineman's foot and the subsequent Travis Henry touchdown, I found myself screaming out loud and breaking into a rather hearty rendition of Rocky Top.

And by the time the Vols got to Sun Devil Stadium and the showdown with Florida State for the BCS title, my temperature—and my blood pressure—was rising like a rocket ship into a night space launch.

On a personal note, I have known Dave Hooker for more than 20 years and have always found him to be one of the finest sports journalists—and people—in our industry. I was deeply touched when he asked me to participate in this wonderful project. And I am convinced that all of you will enjoy this journey back in time to 1998 as much as I did.

—Paul Finebaum
The Paul Finebaum Show
ESPN Radio

CHAPTER 1

The Transfer of Power

The Vols' final two games of the 1997 season set the tone for Tennessee's run at perfection the following year. It began with the birth of a leader at halftime of the SEC Championship Game as the Vols faced getting upset by Auburn. The Vols trailed the Tigers 20-10 when the two teams left the field and headed into the Georgia Dome locker rooms.

"I remember us not playing our best football in the first half. I do remember that very vividly," linebacker Al Wilson said. "I remember going into the locker room at halftime and the vibe just wasn't the vibe we normally had at halftime."

The Vols didn't seem excited for the second half before Wilson spoke up. His fiery speech helped spark a frenetic comeback that secured an SEC title for the Vols for the first time since 1990.

The fire was stoked for 1998.

"Once you win one, you want to continue winning them," Wilson said. "It fueled the fire. It was the fuel that we put on that fire for that 1998 season. Even though we lost so many great players going into the '98 season, we still knew that we had a helluva football team. We still had some players that could really play and some of the best players in the country."

Those players didn't play like the best players in the Orange Bowl after the SEC Championship Game comeback. With a possible national title at stake for Nebraska, the Cornhuskers hammered the Vols 42-17. That was even more fuel for the fire heading into the off season.

"Let's be completely honest," Wilson said, "Nebraska just kicked our butt hands down. They manhandled us. ... That particular game showed us that we had some work to do. In the offseason, we needed to get bigger. We needed to get stronger. We needed to work harder. We needed to be more in tune to what our jobs are. And we needed to hold each other accountable.

"That's the kind of the approach we took into the 1998 season. Everybody do their job because if you don't, we will hold you accountable. We're going to call you out if you're not doing it. That was the beautiful thing about the '98 team. You didn't have to worry about the coaches getting on players for not doing their jobs. It was going to be your teammates that were going to let you know.

"Do your damn job and that's it. Don't try to do too much. Do your job and we'll go from there. That was our approach. That's the love I have for that '98 team because it was strictly business."

Wherever the Vols ended up in 1998, it was clear that Wilson would lead them there.

With a new leader in place and the sting of the Orange Bowl humiliation still resonating, the table was set for one of the most unlikely national title runs in college football history, especially considering how many players the Vols lost from the previous season.

The list of players lost from the 1997 team is astounding. The Vols had eight players drafted by the NFL following the 1997 season, including Peyton Manning, who was the first overall pick. The Vols also lost cornerback Terry Fair and receiver Marcus Nash, who also went in the first round. That was just the beginning.

Defensive linemen Leonard Little and Jonathan Brown were selected in the third round. Offensive lineman Trey Teague and receiver Andy McCullough were selected in the second round.

"No one expected us to win," safety Fred White said. "It was an us-against-the-world mentality. We had all this superstar power the year before, but what they failed to realize is that we worked just as hard. We just hadn't had a chance to play."

The Vols were ranked No. 10 in the preseason AP Poll, but there was no reason to believe they could accomplish more than reaching the SEC Championship Game again in 1998. That was a reasonable goal considering all of the losses. Winning an SEC title seemed a bit lofty. Competing for a national championship wasn't even in the conversation—except for those in Tennessee's locker room.

"We weren't really expected to do that much," former UT Coach Phillip Fulmer said. "It was fun to watch them come together in spring practice. We were having our struggles offensively, but we were a good kicking team and a good defensive team, so we had a chance. As we continued to develop our passing game offensively, the defense kind of carried the load. ... They were selfless and hard workers."

The players on the 1998 team had something to prove in the post-Manning era.

Building a passing game was indeed a struggle. The Vols had to change philosophies completely. Manning had the ability to break down a defense. In essence, he was a coach on the field. His replacement, Tee Martin, was a strong-armed quarterback with the potential to extend plays with his running ability.

"I didn't think we could be what we were with Peyton and I was right," former UT Offensive Coordinator David Cutcliffe said. "I just didn't see that as a remote possibility, but I couldn't put my finger on what we had to do to be special. I think our players helped guide us in that direction, but I had a lot of concerns offensively as we were moving forward."

Said Fulmer, "We couldn't make a first down in spring practice. It was rough. One, our defense was very good."

Tennessee's offense had no consistency during spring practice in 1998. It was, by all accounts, a struggle to move the ball throughout the entire offseason, which included some summer workouts that were more like full practices.

No one needed to tell UT's defensive players that the offense was struggling. The topic came up in a defensive meeting shortly after spring practice.

"We were talking about how we were going to have to play better every game simply because we had a new quarterback," Wilson said. "When you lose Peyton Manning, I don't give a damn who you put in after that, it's not going to be at that level at that point. Tee Martin did a helluva job running the offense and making plays, but he wasn't Peyton Manning. We knew we were going to have to go out and make plays on our side of the ball."

Wilson and his teammates only knew one thing to do with the deck stacked against them. Work, work some more, and work hard. The season was pressing upon them and the doubters were aplenty.

"Coming into that year, there were a lot of red flags," safety Fred White said. "There were a lot of things said about us as a team, that we couldn't get it done without Peyton and we couldn't get it done without those guys. It was a slap in our face because we had been champing at the bit waiting on our chance to get an opportunity to show what we could do. ... No one expected us to win. It was an us-against-the-world mentality.

"It was like we were the replacements. We had all this superstar power the year before, but what they failed to realize is we worked just as hard. We just hadn't had a chance to play. Back then, Tennessee stockpiled recruits. We were just like Alabama today. We had a group of guys that could step in and start for most teams in the country. We felt disrespected so we banded together as a team. That camaraderie and that chemistry was what helped us through all of that."

The Vols headed into summer workouts determined to raise their game to another level. Manning had famously instituted "voluntary" off-season workouts during his career because the NCAA doesn't allow offseason workouts to be mandatory. However, if you wanted to play in the fall, working out in the summer was absolutely mandatory. Tennessee's leaders weren't really worried about the NCAA rulebook at the time.

The 1998 team took Manning's vision to another level. The Vols didn't just hold summer workouts. They held summer practices.

"We were having full blown practices with no pads," White said. "And we were going hard. When we got to practice in the summer, that (pre-season) camp was a breeze. Football season? That was a breeze because we practiced so doggone hard. We demanded perfection."

Perfection meant more than just working out. The Vols had the option to work out in the afternoon or early in the morning. In truth, there was no option.

"If we saw you working out later in the afternoon, we knew you weren't committed," White said. "You're not here with the rest of the team working out in the early morning?"

That philosophy bled into preseason camp. Team leaders would go to UT's coaches and tell them who wasn't practicing hard.

"We all wanted to work hard for our position and we did," White said. "It made us better as football players. It made us closer as teammates and our chemistry was so much different because we saw the hard work everyone put in. If you didn't put in the hard work, we did not want you on our football field. I've got a lot of teammates that I love to death, and I would never say their names, but some of those guys didn't work hard. That's why some of those guys didn't play.

"On our team, if you didn't work hard in practice, you weren't playing—plain and simple. We made sure the coaches knew 'That guy should not be on the football field. I do not want him on our football field because he's not working hard in practice. I see his work ethic and I don't need that on the football field because we need to fight tooth and nail for every inch.' That's what won us a championship."

Despite the boulder the Vols carried on their shoulder, Fulmer thought it might be time for some extra oomph just before the season. He openly challenged his team during UT's annual preseason senior meeting. More than two decades later, defensive tackle Jeff Coleman remembers what Fulmer told the Vols in that meeting.

"I'm looking around and I don't know if we're going to be 7-4 or 6-5," Coleman said, recalling what Fulmer relayed. "When he said it, everybody in the room just looked at each other like, he can't be serious. ... We felt disrespected. We had something to prove. We already had something to prove, but that just really lit a fire under everybody.

"That's the thing I remember most about that year. That's what kind of started it for me. He says he did it as a motivational tool. I think he believed it."

Said Fulmer, "That meeting, I remember, was about leadership. We had lost a lot of leadership. ... I told them all and pointed out a few of them. This is a team you've got to make into what it's going to be. This is what we will be if you don't. It was great, actually, because they responded in a super way."

Wilson and his teammates listened, but they didn't buy into Fulmer's doomsday scenario.

"I don't think anybody in that room believed we would win (just) seven or eight games," Wilson said. "I think we knew we would win more than that, but that was Phillip's way of challenging us."

More challenges were on the horizon.

Al Wilson and Peyton Manning

CHAPTER 2

Replacing a Legend

Fans and media always want more access to their favorite college football teams. What are the coaches really thinking? How is the team performing in practice? That type of access to Tennesse's offense would have been rather uninspiring before the 1998 season.

UT's offense had to be rebuilt following the 1997 season. The entire philosophy of the offense that had thrived for three-plus seasons under Peyton Manning had to be reworked. Manning was gone, as was the tendency for Tennessee's coaches to throw the ball more aggressively with him at the helm. The Vols had to morph into something different on offense.

"I don't think there's any question," former UT Offensive Coordinator David Cutcliffe said of the metamorphosis. "One of the things that we became, we became physical. That 1998 team could run power. We defined that starting in the spring. I think we played a role in our defense becoming maybe the best defense in the country because we went right at them. They beat us and beat us up badly.

"That spring I started to wonder if we'd ever make a first down, but we did not back off."

Tee Martin was tabbed to replace Manning in 1998. Martin admitted that he lacked the consistency his coaches were looking for in spring practice. It wasn't a fun time for anyone, but especially Martin.

"As a competitor, you just want to be good, period," Martin said. "You want to win at everything."

That wasn't happening for Martin or UT's offense as they struggled in the off-season during spring practice and summer workouts. Fortunately,

Tennessee's coaches adapted to Martin's strengths instead of simply running the offense that Manning had mastered.

"Obviously, the whole key of it was what was Tee Martin going to be able to really do," former Tennessee Coach Phillip Fulmer said. "We found a way to make it happen."

UT's coaches decided to lean on some old tricks. They built their offense as it had been under former quarterback Heath Shuler. Like Martin, Shuler was known for his mobility and strong arm. In order to take advantage of Martin's talents, the Vols started exploring ways to move the pocket and ran more naked bootlegs and waggles.

"We used some of those plays and systems to fit Tee," Fulmer said. "Tee was more like Heath than he was Peyton—for sure early."

Martin wasn't the only concern on UT's offense headed into the 1998 season. The Vols had to make adjustments on the offensive line, figure out how to handle the rotation of a talented group of tailbacks, and replace two receivers who were selected in the NFL Draft. It wasn't an easy challenge and the first matchup was daunting as the Vols were scheduled to play No. 15 Syracuse on the road.

"Fall camp was a little frightening," Cutcliffe said. "I wasn't sure we were ready to go to Syracuse and be successful offensively against a good Syracuse football team. We had already made a commitment to our offensive line and our backs. We lived with it."

UT's offense also lived with daily beatdowns in practice. The Vols' defense never took it easy on their offensive counterparts just because they played on the same team. Former UT linebacker Al Wilson chuckled when he was asked about the offense's struggles heading into the 1998 season.

"It was tough for the offense. I'll say that," Wilson said. "We had one of the best defenses in the country so we didn't make it easy on them. We took it very seriously to go out and compete with them because at the end of the day, if they can move the ball on us, they can move the ball on anybody in the country. That's the way we felt.

"It wasn't about going out and taking it easy. It was about going out and competing and making these guys play football on the other side. They had some damn good football players over there. If we can make it tough on them in practice, then it should be a lot easier for them on Saturday."

Martin had waited too long behind Manning to wilt. He relished the opportunity to face UT's defense in practice. It was the ultimate test.

"There wasn't a defense that we faced that season that from top to bottom could play man, could play zone, could pressure you, could stop the run, could take away your best wideouts in the passing game," Martin said. "I thought (defensive coordinator) John Chavis did a really good job of positioning the talent on our defense to be successful for his scheme. ... I really feel though that defense was intelligent and talented and that's what made them what they were."

That mindset was brought on by the former leaders UT had, such as Manning and Defensive End Leonard Little, among others. Hard work was the only way the Vols could overcome the many personnel losses from the previous season. Hard work? The 1998 Vols were used to that from previous seasons.

"There were a lot of lessons learned by our players about commitment to football and work ethic," Cutcliffe said. "I've told Peyton and those guys that they had a lot to do with that national championship. No doubt in my mind."

Certainly, Manning left the foundation, but the football was ultimately in another man's hands in 1998. And that man wasn't content with being babied early in the season.

CHAPTER 3

Tee's Time

Tee Martin had plenty of reasons to choose Tennessee after a fantastic career at Williamson High School in Mobile, Alabama. However, there was one big reason not to sign with the Vols.

Let's start with the positives. By choosing UT over Notre Dame and Auburn, Martin would be playing for a bona fide winning program with some of the best tradition in the nation. He also would get to learn from Offensive Coordinator David Cutcliffe, who was quickly being considered as one of the best offensive minds in the country. Those are all pretty positive reasons to become a Vol.

However, there was one really big reason not to choose Tennessee. That reason was Peyton Manning.

Choosing UT meant Martin would be sitting behind Manning for at least one season and possibly two if Manning didn't enter the NFL Draft following his junior season in 1996. Martin was not daunted by waiting—even after Manning shocked the college football world with his decision to return for his senior season in 1997.

"That was part of the whole respect that he earned," former UT coach Phillip Fulmer said of Martin. "He could have easily made some noise. I think everyone was somewhat surprised that Peyton stayed in school and passed on being the first pick (in the NFL Draft). He wanted to enjoy another year, which we were fortunate and it was great that he did.

"Tee had to bite the bullet and he did. He was not a guy that complained at all. He knew he would get his opportunities. Instead of three years, he had two really great years. It was hard for him I'm sure."

Tee Martin

Not too hard. Sure, like any competitor, Martin would have liked to play more. But instead of complaining in 1997, he continued with the approach that led him to Knoxville, to face off against an elite signal caller.

"The reason why I chose to come (to UT) was to compete with Manning, who I felt was the best college quarterback," Martin said. "I could have gone other places and started as a true freshman and who knows what that would have been like. When I found out how good (Manning) was, I said, 'Man, how could you prove yourself to be one of the better ones if you don't compete against the best one every day?'

"I didn't know if I would sit for one year or two years. It ended up being two years, but I was OK with that. It was just a competitive challenge for me to show and prove to the coaching staff and my teammates that I belong."

When Manning finally left following the 1997 season, it was Martin's turn to lead UT's offense. While some other players might have tried to live up to Manning's legacy or even surpass it, Martin didn't view the transition that way.

"It wasn't a personal vendetta," Martin said. "I wanted to go against the best defense in the SEC (in practice at UT) and actually perform well against them. I wanted to show (receiver) Peerless Price, the receiving corps, (running back) Jamal Lewis, and the offensive line that I could make the checks at the line of scrimmage, I could get us in the right play, I can take care of the football, and get the ball in the end zone. Those are things that I focused on. It never really motivated me to fill the shoes of Peyton."

Martin never had to fight for his teammates' respect. It was always there. However, his coaches' confidence was another matter. Martin admitted that he grew frustrated at times when his coaches scaled back the offense in 1998, even if it did make sense. Martin was a first-year starter, the Vols were a power-running football team in 1998 and could lean on a stout defense and consistent special teams play. Yet Martin believed he could do more.

The Vols knew early they had to rely on running the football, some occasional play-action passes, and Martin's running ability to extend plays, which was a trait that Manning never had. Cutcliffe will always be known for his work with the Mannings—Peyton and his brother Eli Manning.

Tee Martin

Both quarterbacks had Hall of Fame careers and multiple Super Bowl victories. However, the way Cutcliffe handled the transition to Martin was masterful.

"We had a relationship where he allowed me to be myself," Martin said of Cutcliffe. "Filling the shoes of Peyton before me, you can't replace or try to emulate that. You have to go in and be yourself. Those are the conversations that we had going into the season. It was about being a consistent performer."

Fate forced UT's hand a bit after running back Jamal Lewis was knocked out for the season with a knee injury in the Auburn game. The Vols, then 4-0, couldn't continue to be so simplistic in the passing game without Lewis on the field.

The Vols faced No. 7 Georgia the following week after Lewis was injured in Athens. Martin completed 16-of-22 for 156 yards and three touchdowns. He also ran for 107 yards. Martin and UT's passing offense was a growing, more-efficient threat as the season rolled on.

"After the Georgia game, we became a more complete passing team," Fulmer said.

That became obvious when the Vols faced South Carolina on Halloween. Martin's accuracy was at an all-time high when he set an NCAA record with 24 consecutive completions. Martin finished the Alabama game with a completion the week before he completed 23 consecutive passes against the Gamecocks. The Vols easily won 49-14.

As Martin's efficiency grew, his explosiveness never waned. He was always a threat to run the football, and his connection to Peerless Price resulted in several downfield touchdowns.

Peerless Price

Tee Martin

"Big plays to receivers along with that run game made a huge difference," Cutcliffe said.

Those deep passes from Martin seemed to crop up just when the Vols needed them. There was the 29-yard touchdown midway through the third quarter against the Gators. Trailing Mississippi State 14-10 in the fourth quarter of the SEC Championship Game, Martin threw two touchdown passes in 32 seconds in the fourth quarter to take the lead. The first was a 41-yard strike to Price. The second was a 26-yard pass to Cedrick Wilson after a State fumble. And no Tennessee fan can forget the 76-yard touchdown pass to Price that put the Vols up 20-9 in the Fiesta Bowl against Florida State. That play practically sealed a national title for the Vols.

Martin was never in the hunt for the Heisman Trophy like Manning, nor was Martin ever considered to be the first overall pick in the NFL Draft like Manning. That was one of the keys to the 1998 season: Martin never tried to be like Manning.

In the process, Martin took the Vols to heights Manning couldn't, but none of that would have happened had it not been for an upset on a muggy September night in a series that was getting downright unbearable for the Vols.

CHAPTER 4

The Early Challenges

Of course, no one was aware of the Vols' mindset when the season kicked off. No one knew that Tennessee had a bunch of hungry, perhaps angry, players that didn't think they should be overlooked just because they lost a ton of talent, including a Manning.

The Vols were ranked No. 10 in the Associated Press Preseason Poll. Finishing 10th would have been an accomplishment with an opening road trip to No. 17 Syracuse and a daunting SEC schedule ahead. However, the bond and chemistry that developed during all of that off-season work had the Vols shooting for much more when the season started. The first test came immediately.

Syracuse had one of its best teams in years, led by future NFL star quarterback Donovan McNabb. The Vols also found the Syracuse's homefield a bit inhospitable. Perhaps because of all the intense off-season conditioning, cramping was an issue even in the first half of the game in the Carrier Dome.

"It always amazes me that the largest air-conditioning company is Carrier," said Randy Sanders, who coached running backs to begin the season. "Then you go to the Carrier Dome and it's not air-conditioned."

UT trailed Syracuse 33-31 late in the game. It appeared Syracuse had won when Martin's pass to Cedrick Wilson fell incomplete on 4th-and-7. Then, a flag flew in. Syracuse cornerback Will Allen was called for pass interference, which gave the Vols a first down.

"I remember when it happened I thought it was pass interference," said Sanders, who was standing nearby on the sideline. "My biggest concern—was the official going to call that on fourth down on the road? Obviously it was the right call, but officials are human. It takes courage to make the right call on fourth down on the road."

With a second life, the Vols drove to the 10-yard line. Kicker Jeff Hall kicked a 27-yard field goal as time expired to steal a victory, 34-33. One down. Twelve to go.

Jeff Hall

The Vols hosted No. 2 Florida after a bye week. It seemed likely the Gators would win. Florida, rather famously and boisterously, had beaten UT five consecutive times, the latter four largely against Manning.

"There for a while, it seemed like even when we had the better team for a few years, Florida still had our number," Sanders said.

Not this time. The Vols' defense made sure of that.

Florida QB Jesse Palmer being tackled by Tennessee S Fred White

"Going into that game, we already knew it wasn't going to be a super high-scoring game," Wilson said. "They didn't have a super explosive offense ... but we knew that Florida had a helluva defense. We knew that defensively it was going to come down to us on our side of the ball to win that football game.

"After losing to them for three straight years (in my career), we were just determined not to lose. It was that simple. It was one of those mind-sets that we're not going to lose four in a row."

Wilson was right. Steve Spurrier's Gators outgained the Vols 396 to 235 yards, but the Gators had five turnovers. Wilson forced three fumbles, which is a school record. Fullback Shawn Bryson scored on a 57-yard touchdown run in the first quarter. The Vols also scored on a 29-yard touchdown pass from Martin to receiver Peerless Price.

The game was hard fought before Hall nailed a 41-yard field goal to help beat the Gators 20-17 after Florida kicker Collins Cooper's field goal attempt sailed wide left in overtime.

Post-game celebration in Neyland Stadium after Tennessee beat Florida in 1998

The Vols were 2-0. They had survived cramps in the Carrier Dome, a pass that initially looked incomplete, and the dreaded Gators. The Vols had every goal left to play for, and it looked like it the next time they took the field.

The Vols hammered Houston 42-7 the following week before returning to SEC play. Auburn was next—a rematch of the SEC Championship Game.

Still struggling to find more offensive production, UT's defense ruled the day on The Plains. Defensive lineman Shaun Ellis was named the SEC Defensive Player of the Week thanks, in part, to a 90-yard interception return for a touchdown. Running back Jamal Lewis ran for 67 yards and a touchdown on his first carry. The Vols also turned in a key goal-line stand with Wilson, who was injured, cheering on his teammates from the sideline.

"Being a leader, I had to stay in tune to the football game, so when the defense is on the field, I was looking at the opposing offense, looking at formations, looking at motions and trying to figure this is what they're trying to do to us," Wilson said. "So when the guys came back to the sideline, it's like having another coach on the field with you."

The Vols beat Auburn 17-9, but it was far from a perfect day. Lewis suffered a season-ending knee injury. That was an incredible gut punch for the Vols.

Lewis had been the focal point of a UT offense that was still trying to find its identity. His loss wouldn't be easy to overcome. However, the Vols couldn't mope; they had to adapt. A date at No. 7 Georgia was seven days away.

The Vols responded incredibly well without Lewis. Travis Stephens rushed for 107 yards and Travis Henry ran for 53 yards as UT beat Georgia 22-3 in Athens.

"We were a huge underdog," Fulmer said. "At that time we were still undefeated and an underdog. That shocked us. They were a good team but certainly a team we had beaten at home the year before pretty good. I think our guys got pretty pumped up to play. It was a

Jamal Lewis

pivotal game for us. ... We beat them a lot worse than the score was. I do know that."

The Georgia win infused the Vols with confidence. They could win without Lewis, and the passing game was more than just screens and an occasional deep pass. Beating the Bulldogs as soundly as they did was also personal for several Vols as many key UT players hailed from Georgia, such as White, offensive lineman Cosey Coleman, and safety Deon Grant. Beating Georgia handily was a midseason bonus for the players from the Peach Tree State.

The remainder of the opponents on Tennessee's schedule seemed beatable. There were plenty of big-name programs left, but no one seemed to be a major threat immediately after the Georgia game. However, there was a formidable foe that was gaining steam just like the Vols. They wore red, but it wasn't Alabama.

As odd as it might seem now, the Vols cruised past the Crimson Tide, as they were used to. UT beat the Tide 35-18 to notch its fourth consecutive win over its rival.

The offense had found its stride.

The Vols then crushed South Carolina 49-14 and UAB 37-13. Tennessee was 8-0—already exceeding Fulmer's preseason skepticism. They climbed to No. 1 in the AP Poll—the first time since 1956. The road seemed paved to the SEC Championship Game.

Tennessee showed a maturity in that run of games following Georgia that no one would have expected with a team that lost so much leadership from the previous season. The Vols were better than the teams they played and showed it. UT didn't need a key pass-interference call, a rash of opposing turnovers, or a goal-line stand to beat Bama, South Carolina, and UAB.

They just needed to play like they had practiced in the long off-season leading up to the 1998 season. However, there was one major hurdle to overcome and it would determine the Vols' fate.

That 'other' red team was intent on ruining the Vols' season of perfection.

Al WIlson

CHAPTER 5

Finishing the Run

As surprising as UT's 1998 season was, Arkansas was nearly as stunning. Like the Vols, the Razorbacks were undefeated and hoping for a shot at an SEC and national title. The two teams were set for an epic matchup in Neyland Stadium. The game certainly lived up to its billing.

Tennessee trailed Arkansas 24-10 in the third quarter. The Razorbacks, ranked No. 10, seemed as though they were putting the game away in the fourth quarter. They led 24-22 and were driving. One first down would end the game. That's when an unlikely event happened and a hero appeared.

"A miracle," Coleman told reporters after the game.

Defensive tackle Billy Ratliff decided he'd take things into his own hands with the season on the line against Arkansas. He famously told Martin to keep his helmet handy because UT's defense would get the ball back. Ratliff, who admittedly had been beaten throughout the game by Arkansas All-American Offensive guard Brandon Burlsworth, decided to jump the snap, risk jumping offsides, and just try to make a play.

"I stuck my arm straight in his chest and was going to try to drive him into the goalpost," Ratliff said.

Arkansas quarterback Clint Stoerner was pressured when Ratliff drove Burlsworth into Stoerner, causing him to stumble. Stoerner seemingly placed the ball on the ground as he tried to balance himself. Ratliff jumped on the loose ball, giving Tennessee an unexpected opportunity.

After taking over at the Hogs' 43-yard line with just 1:43 left, the Vols wouldn't be denied. Henry ran the ball five consecutive times. The final run resulted in a one-yard touchdown run with 28 seconds left and an eventual 28-24 win.

Al Wilson

Travis Henry

According to many players and coaches on the 1998 team, that sequence of events made them believe they were destined to be national champions. The Vols had tasted what it was like to lose even in a win. They didn't like that taste.

The Vols blew by Kentucky 59-21, then hammered Vanderbilt 41-0.

Next up was a shot at winning UT's second consecutive SEC title. All the Vols had to do was beat No. 23 Mississippi State. That proved more difficult than many expected.

The Vols trailed Mississippi State 14-10 before Martin threw two touchdown passes in 32 seconds in the fourth quarter. The first was a 41-yard strike to Price. The second was a 26-yard pass to Wilson after a State fumble. It was a sign of how far UT's offense had come.

The Vols could still run the ball, but Martin was now considered a threat in the passing game. He never doubted he could do it. Cutcliffe, however, thought it best to keep the reins tight on the passing game, especially early in the season. Martin wasn't pleased with that approach.

"I had frustrating moments during that year where I knew I could do more, but I wasn't getting the opportunity to do more," Martin said.

Throughout the regular season, Martin had proven himself to Tennessee's coaching staff.

The Vols could do more on offense and the biggest stage was yet to come. Tennessee had taken care of its regular season and conference chores. The Vols were 12-0.

Tennessee was ranked No. 1 in the major polls and—most important—in the all-new BCS ranking. It was the first year of the BCS system that used an equation to determine the top two teams that would play in the national championship game. Thanks to losses by the nation's other two undefeated teams, UCLA and Kansas State, the Vols were assured a chance to win a national title. They would face Florida State in the Fiesta Bowl in Tempe, Arizona.

However, the Vols had another challenge to endure before heading west to try to secure the first national title for Tennessee in 47 years.

Cutcliffe had interviewed with Ole Miss and was expected to leave to become the Rebels' head coach. Once he was officially offered the job,

Tee Martin

Tee Martin

Darwin Walker

the question was when Cutcliffe would leave. Ole Miss asked him to coach in the Independence Bowl against Texas Tech. Cutcliffe knew he couldn't be in both places at once, so he decided to leave UT and take on the Ole Miss challenge. Cutcliffe, who is now the head coach at Duke, had coached at UT since 1982. The emotions were strong.

"I cried in front of that team," Cutcliffe said, recalling telling his players. "I cried at home, literally cried. I grieved."

Cutcliffe said there were two reasons he agreed to leave immediately for Ole Miss. First, he felt confident in Sanders as UT's offensive coordinator. Second, Cutcliffe felt confident in his team.

"There was no way on God's green Earth they weren't going to win that game," Cutcliffe said. "I never had a concern."

Most of the sports world didn't agree with Cutcliffe. Most predicted a Florida State victory despite the fact that the Seminoles had to play their third-string quarterback, Marcus Outzen, due to injuries to starter Chris Weinke and backup Jared Jones.

Florida State's best offensive threat was Receiver Peter Warrick, who also starred as a punt returner. Defensive back Dwayne Goodrich knew what he had to do. He made it clear to Defensive Backs Coach Kevin Ramsey.

"I told Coach Ramsey I wanted Peter Warrick wherever he went the whole game," Goodrich said.

The strategy worked. Goodrich and the Vols contained Warrick. More important, Goodrich jumped one of Warrick's routes and returned an Outzen interception 54 yards for a touchdown.

"I knew he couldn't run by me," Goodrich said. "He wasn't faster than me, so I wasn't worried about him blowing by me."

That put the Vols in control. However, they'd need one more big play to secure UT's first national title in 47 years. Tennessee receiver Peerless Price was ready.

"I'll never forget that play call," said Sanders, who took over for Cutcliffe as Tennessee's offensive coordinator. "It was '69 Go.' Florida State had a huge tendency. They either played Cover 2 or they played man-to-man in those situations. It was a route that was good versus either of those coverages. We felt good about Peerless. Peerless had a great game for us. He kind of got hot. Tee had a lot of confidence in it. One of the things Tee did very well was throw the deep ball."

Price hauled in a 79-yard touchdown pass that gave the Vols a 20-9 lead midway through the fourth quarter. That was all UT's defense would need. Florida State tacked on a late touchdown, but the perfect Vols stayed perfect, 23-16.

Fiesta Bowl Final Score

"The SEC titles were good; the national championship was a feeling that I never could have imagined," Wilson said. "That national title puts you as the creme de la creme. You are the number uno in college football. ... That's a feeling that's indescribable."

And it was all born out of the hard work that began a year earlier and the chemistry that resulted in a dedication to being a team.

"Nobody expected that '98 team to be that special," Wilson said. "That's why I believe we were so much closer as a team simply because nobody gave us a chance. That just motivated guys to go out and want to play hard and compete for each other and show the world that we're a lot better than you think we are. That's what stood out to me, how close we were as a team, the way we hung together off the field, the way we held each other accountable when guys weren't doing their job.

"The way we policed ourselves other than as a team. Coaches didn't have to worry about us off the field. We did it ourselves. If a guy is out fucking up, you pull him to the side and let him know we need everybody doing their role and doing their part."

That bond was unbreakable. It has survived decades and a prison sentence in which one former Vol really effed up.

CHAPTER 6

Overcoming Tragedy

Tennessee didn't just win a national championship in 1998 with all of those off-season workouts. They didn't just win a title with all of those reps in the weight room. Tennessee's players built a bond that would overcome a disastrous accident caused by one of its key players.

Dwayne Goodrich was one of the few players on Tennessee's team that wasn't from the South. The cornerback from Richards High School in Oak Lawn, Illinois, was proof that the Vols recruited nationally and weren't afraid to step in anyone else's recruiting footprint.

Goodrich became a star at Tennessee. He was selected to the All-SEC team twice during his career in Knoxville. He was also selected to various All-American lists during his senior season in which he had six interceptions. There was little doubt that Goodrich would have a substantial—if not long—career in the NFL. He had stood toe-to-toe with the best receivers in the nation and won most of those battles.

That would never happen.

Goodrich was selected in the second round of the NFL Draft by the Dallas Cowboys. He had big shoes to fill as the Cowboys were looking for a cornerback to replace Deion Sanders, who was expected to move on from Dallas. Be it pressure or youth, Goodrich made a horrible decision in January 2003. That decision would cost Goodrich his career and, more importantly, the lives of two good Samaritans.

Goodrich served six years in prison following a traffic accident in which he was convicted of criminally negligent homicide and failure to render aid in the deaths of two men. Goodrich was charged with vehicular manslaughter when he was involved in a hit-and-run accident that killed

Dwayne Goodrich

two people that were trying to aid a man in a burning car on the freeway in the middle of the night. Goodrich fled the scene after an evening of hitting the clubs.

An emotional embrace with the lone surviving victim was the last time Goodrich was seen before being hauled off to prison.

Once in prison, Goodrich disappeared.

"It was tough because we tried to set up a thing to go see him and visit him and he said 'no,'" former UT safety Fred White said. "I remember him saying 'I don't want you all to come see me because when you all leave I have to stay.' He didn't need that emotional situation.

"I'm not going to lie. That hurt. That's a brother. You want to be there for your brother and we couldn't. You know the person. You know the man he is."

Even while accepting all blame, the burden was incredible to bear for Goodrich. However, he chose to do so on his own. Other than his closest family members, no one could contact Goodrich directly. All correspondence went through his mother.

"For me, I had to mature mentally and understand how to deal with that first before I had guys reach out to me," Goodrich said. "I pushed a lot of people away, just until I understood what I was going through. I had to understand how to forgive myself first. ... I was embarrassed. I didn't really know how to deal with the negative attention."

Goodrich was released from the Wallace Unit of the Texas Correctional System in Colorado City, Texas, in 2011. He decided to reach out to his fellow defensive back. Willing to cover his back, White helped out his former teammate.

"I was so happy to have him back," White said. "It was amazing. My boys are my family. That was my brother. I got my brother back."

The two shared a one-bedroom apartment in Knoxville. Goodrich slept on the couch until they could find something more suitable. Goodrich came back to Knoxville with a purpose. He was determined to finish his degree. As he rearranged his life on White's couch, Goodrich knew he had support.

"My entire Vol family, they've always been there—even for me getting back to school and finishing up," Goodrich said. "Those guys were 110-percent supportive of my journey, the good and the bad, over the last twenty years."

Goodrich wasn't the only former Vol in that one-bedroom apartment who was thinking about the future. His determination rubbed off.

"If he had not come back to Knoxville, I don't know if I would have gone back to school. I had given up on the notion of going back," White said. "People say I helped Dwayne. I didn't help Dwayne. We helped each other. He lit a fire under me and changed my thought process."

Goodrich and White graduated from UT following the spring semester in 2014.

Goodrich is now an active member of the 1998 alum group that won a national title. What made that bond so strong? There was one central figure that no one would debate led the Vols to an elite level on the field and as a family...

CHAPTER 7

A Legendary Leader

It would be tough to find a player that better embodied the 1998 Volunteers than linebacker Al Wilson, who was known for being tough, athletic, and just a bit surly.

It doesn't take long to be around Wilson and see that if a fight breaks out, you want him on your side. Wilson played high school football at Jackson-Central Merry in Jackson, Tennessee, where he starred at linebacker and running back.

Tennessee had a habit of taking great skill-position athletes and putting them at linebacker. It mostly worked, but sometimes it didn't. There's a difference between being hit and hitting someone else. There was never a question that Wilson was going to play linebacker even though he was recruited as a safety. At either position, Wilson liked to hit—a lot.

Wilson's hitting was a huge part of his game. That, along with his intensity, led to two All-Pro selections in the NFL and five Pro Bowls. Coaches want talent, passion, and strong work ethic all wrapped up in one. That's what Wilson was. However, the void he filled in 1998 was more important than just taking care of a gap. After four years of Manning being the face of the Vols, someone had to step up when Manning went on to a Hall of Fame career. That's what Wilson did.

Wilson was known for his leadership in 1998. It was born in 1997 when the Vols were about to let a championship slip through their fingers in Atlanta. No one asked Wilson to take control at halftime of that SEC Championship Game when Auburn was about to dash the Vols' championship dreams. No one needed to ask. Once considered one of Tennessee's quiet players, Wilson roared to life in the locker room and challenged his teammates.

"He became Al Wilson that you know as the leader in the locker room against Auburn in the SEC Championship Game in 1997," former UT safety Fred White said. "For all the guys on the team, we already saw that leadership skill that he had. That night, it was like a changing of the guard."

The previous regime of Vol leadership was headed by quarterback Peyton Manning and defensive end Leonard Little. It was formidable, but it wasn't Wilson.

"They were leaders," White said of Manning and Little. "However, that night the leaders needed to be quiet and shut up and let a young guy like Al step in and say 'Man, this is it.' He gave us the business that night. ... What he said, everybody stopped to listen because all you had seen is that guy work his butt off. That was the right time for him to become the leader and show you he was the leader. When he did, you had to listen because he had never really said anything."

Wilson wasn't afraid to call out Manning or Little that night. He also wasn't afraid to reminisce on the halftime fireworks that he set afire. Wilson said that it seemed no one was excited to take the field in the second half as the Vols usually were. That wasn't acceptable.

"Nobody was really standing up and saying anything," Wilson said. "Me being a guy that is emotional and passionate about the game of football, I had never won a championship at anything before in my life. Maybe at the YMCA at basketball when I was like seven or eight years old, but other than that I had never won a championship before. That was the closest I had ever been to becoming a winner and becoming a champion.

"I just felt like if any time is going to be the right time to stand up and say something, now is the time. I challenged Leonard. I challenged Peyton. I challenged everybody on the team to go out in the second half and let's turn this thing around and see what happens. We'll let the chips fall where they may, but we've got to go out and play better football in the second half. Everybody has to do their job. ... I just told him and Leonard, 'You

Peyton Manning

guys are our leaders. Lead us.' I remember specifically calling those two guys out. It was that simple."

Keep in mind who Wilson was calling out. Manning was a strong Heisman contender. Little was a rare combination of size and athleticism that allowed him to play middle linebacker and defensive end in college. Still, Wilson called it "simple."

The fiery, simple approach worked. UT outscored Auburn 20-9 in the second half to notch a 30-29 win and the Vols' first SEC Championship since 1990.

White remembers when he once caught Wilson's ire. White held up to make sure not to hit a ball carrier as he was headed toward the sideline. Wilson didn't like that.

"He grabbed me by the back of my jersey and pulled me all the way to the sideline because he went by me," White said. "He said to me, 'If I ever pass you again going to a ball, we're going to fight right here on this football field.'"

White, who was known as a tough, hard-hitting safety, had no desire to tangle with Wilson.

"I know one thing about him," White said of the prospects of fighting Wilson. "He's going to give it everything he has. He's going to fight to the end. He's going to go 100 percent all out. He's not going to give up. That's not a guy I want to fight."

Wilson's leadership continued little more than a month later when the Vols returned from Tempe, Arizona. The Vols were hammered by Nebraska 42-17 in the Fiesta Bowl. Wilson wasn't happy about that and knew that the Vols needed to squeeze every ounce of effort out of the 1998 team in the off-season considering how many players the Vols would lose from the 1997 team, which included eight NFL Draft picks.

As soon as the Vols returned to Knoxville after the Nebraska debacle, Wilson was ready to sling some iron and challenge other guys to do the same.

"We come back and he's the first guy in the weight room," White said. "Not only is he the first guy, but he's on the phone calling guys, 'Get your butt over here. Let's go.'"

Wilson's leadership style evolved. He learned that screaming at every teammate wasn't the only way to lead.

"I started to see and understand what leadership was really all about, how to approach the leadership role, and one thing that really stood out to me that I learned over the years was the ability to lead each player individually," Wilson said. "It's not a one-size-fits-all type of thing."

Tennessee's coaching staff saw Wilson's leadership ability and felt it was important to encourage it in order to reach their full potential in 1998. Whenever leadership was brought up in team meetings, Wilson believed that Fulmer's message was meant for one man.

"He was speaking to me indirectly and I took exactly what he was saying to heart," Wilson said. "I felt like Coach was counting on me to be that one missing piece that we needed as a team, to stand up when players weren't feeling quite like they wanted to practice that day or guys didn't feel like they wanted to work out that day.

"You always have to have that one guy that's not only going to try to push you along but is going to lead you by example. That was the challenge I took from what Phillip told me in one of those early meetings."

Said White, "You saw how hard he worked and he waited his turn to be the leader. You saw that leadership ability he had every day in practice. He went to work, kept his head down, and when the older guys spoke, he listened and he paid attention. Then he relayed the message to the other guys."

Wilson had to wait to be a leader, but he didn't have to wait long to become embedded with Tennessee's football team, which is the first step. The first bonds Wilson made were developed in Gatlinburg when then-defensive tackle Spencer Riley invited Wilson and White to take a trip to the tourist mecca of East Tennessee.

"I had never even heard of Gatlinburg," White said, looking back on the trip.

Riley, who would end up being the starting center for the Vols throughout the 1998 season, took Wilson and White to ride go-carts and play video games shortly after they arrived on campus. Then, Riley took a gander at one of the bungee jumps that are strewn about the area.

"I'll go, if you go," Riley recalled saying at the time.

So, it was on. All three future champions made the climb up the crane-like structure to test their bravery—or lack of good judgment. Once the three agreed to jump, there was no going back. Riley didn't even hesitate so the onus was quickly on White and Wilson. They knew this wasn't just fun. It was a statement that they weren't scared—of anything.

"You definitely would have never lived that down, that's for sure," Riley said with a big smile. "A lot of things we did during that time we probably shouldn't have done, but we lived to tell about it."

Wilson took about twenty minutes to get up his nerve before jumping. It was a process.

"Don't rush me," he emphatically told Riley and White.

Eventually, Wilson jumped and so did White. It was their first weekend on campus and a brotherhood was born through a thick band of rubber and throwing caution to the wind.

"At that moment, that was our bond," White said. "We've had that bond ever since."

Jumping from a fifty-foot tower was tough. However, the bond that was built at that time would pay huge dividends when Wilson faced a challenge much tougher than anything he'd find on the football field.

In 2009, the toughest guy in UT cleats saw his son diagnosed with brain cancer at just fifteen years old.

"I've been blessed to have an amazing son," Wilson said. "Going through the cancer thing was tougher than anything I've ever experienced. It was tougher than going against any fullback, any offensive lineman, playing any team. It was the toughest thing I could ever be a part of. Just to see him fight through that, push through it and not complain and just do it, whatever it takes to make it through.

"It was an eye-opening experience for me. It was motivating for me. It made me have more of an appreciation for life and understand exactly what my role is in this world."

Carrington overcame cancer and graduated from Triveca University, where he played baseball. At the time of this printing, he is pursuing a medical degree.

"He's an amazing kid," Wilson said. "I couldn't ask for a better child. I'm just happy that I have him in my life."

There are countless Vols that could say the same about the elder Wilson's presence in their lives. Without him, UT's national title run would have likely never taken place. The Vols needed a leader at various points that season, but they also needed a generational kind of play to overcome their most-hated SEC foe.

CHAPTER 8

The Interception

One of the most impactful, most athletic, most memorable plays in Tennessee football history was a trick, a ruse, and an incredible trap laid by one of the best combos of safeties in the history of SEC football.

Tennessee coaches were only slightly aware that safety Deon Grant was trying to trick the Florida Gators when he lined up just far enough to his left to make everyone think that there would be a gaping hole in Tennessee's defensive backfield in September of 1998. Surely, then-Florida Coach Steve Spurrier saw where Grant was lined up. So did former Florida quarterback Jesse Palmer, who had to think he had an easy touchdown pass for the taking.

Palmer threw the ball with confidence to a streaking Nafis Kareem, who had gotten behind Vols' cornerback Derrick Edmonds. In a millisecond, those in attendance with a complete view of the defensive backfield had that same old feeling. Florida was going to score a clutch touchdown in the fourth quarter with the game tied 17-17 and beat Tennessee for the sixth consecutive time.

Good night, game over.

However, that sinking feeling didn't last long as Grant covered nearly half the field to nab Palmer's pass with one hand, with Kareem behind him waiting to snag the ball and streak the rest of the way for a go-ahead score. Sure, Tennessee could have come back and still beaten the Gators, but that was not the way the series tended to play out as the Vols were most oftentimes finding ways to lose to Florida.

The Vols had lost by a combined score of 202-120 in the previous five seasons as Tennessee always seemed to play its worst against the

Gators, who seemed to either just be better or more fortunate repeatedly against Tennessee. Either way, it would take a spectacular play to turn the series.

Grant's interception was as good a catch as has ever been made in Neyland Stadium. The pass was slightly underthrown, but more importantly, it was proof that the Gators could be overthrown as the best of the SEC East. Grant was run out of bounds just shy of Florida territory with the ball firmly in hand. The play would have been magnificent in any game. It was unforgettable because it was against Florida.

"As far as going up for a one-handed catch, that was something I liked to do in practice all the time," Grant said. "Fred and Al and them would tell you that. There was definitely excitement there. There was also some surprise that I was able to get over there and make that play because I didn't realize that Travis was that far away from me and I thought I had held the disguise too long, to be honest with you."

The disguise was the ultimate example of a few things. First, it was visual proof that Tennessee's coaches had faith in the Vols' defenders to improvise. It was also proof that Tennessee's duo of safeties, White and Grant, had an eerie chemistry that would allow White to lock down on opposing offenses when they tried to run the ball because Grant was always the ultimate saving grace lined up in the defensive backfield.

Amongst a team that had complete trust in one another, no player was more trusted than Grant. Had he blown that one play or countless others, the Vols wouldn't have been hoisting a national championship trophy following the 1998 season. It would have been another season of regret embodied most in a loss to Florida in September. However, the play was emblematic of another Tennessee trait.

It was remarkable that the Vols had no fear against Florida in 1998 considering how the series had unfolded. One could have made a strong argument that the Vols should have played more conservatively against Florida in previous years. Perhaps relying more on a running game instead of Manning would have achieved better results. The Vols had no choice but to be pass-happy against Florida in 1998. Tennessee's offense wasn't ready for that after Peyton Manning had moved on to the NFL. However, Tennessee wasn't conservative in its mindset on defense. It was all about attacking.

One could argue that Grant shouldn't have been gambling with the game on the line. With less than seven minutes left in a 17-17 game, it was a pretty aggressive move to try to trick one of the best offenses in SEC history. It clearly could have resulted in another Florida fiasco.

Grant will readily admit that Tennessee's coaches were only slightly aware of what was going on during the famous interception that forever changed SEC football history. The coaches? Well, they didn't really need to know—just as long as Grant's cohort at safety, Fred White, was on the same page—even though it was never discussed between the two.

"We never talked about it," Grant said. "We just had a feeling off of each other. That was one where the strength of my game came into play as far as trying to throw the quarterback off. That's what I was trying to do and I was able to do that by holding the disguise. If I would have lined up in the middle of the field, he never would have thrown that pass."

Tennessee's defensive coaches, led by Coordinator John Chavis, allowed the Vols to freelance. However, Grant was seemingly so far out of position that things were certainly a bit uncomfortable for the Vols' top brass.

"I probably had them scared for a minute," Grant said with a giggle. "I definitely had them scared but at the end, they were probably pretty happy with the outcome."

Here's the craziest aspect of that play: Grant had never tried to pull off such a disguise in college. He had pulled off that sort of disguise before, but not since high school. Grant, on his own, thought it was best to pull out his risky maneuver midway through the fourth quarter against Tennessee's hated rival that had dominated the series. High stakes?

No question. The loser of the Tennessee-Florida game in the 1990's was usually relegated to being second in the SEC East, not in the SEC Championship Game, and no factor in a pending national championship. Essentially, Tennessee's seasons had been crushed by the Gators over and over and over. The 1998 season was supposed to just be another chapter in that tortuous book for Tennessee fans. Tennessee was conservative offensively against Florida in 1998, but there was nothing conservative about Grant's gamble.

As many things as could be said about that play and that defense, it proved that the Vols didn't lack confidence. That play, which lasted about twenty seconds, proved the Vols weren't scared of anyone and further instilled that belief. If the Vols could stand toe-to-toe against their arch-nemesis, what could stop Tennessee for the rest of the season? As it turned out, nothing.

Strangely enough, Grant's interception would have never happened had it not been for some questionable recruiting by former Georgia Coach Ray Goff. He wasn't nearly as high on future star running back Jamal Lewis as he was with a prospect named Jasper Sanks, who would eventually sign with Georgia. That didn't sit well with Grant or a highly rated offensive lineman named Cosey Coleman so he, Grant, and Lewis signed with the Vols instead of the Bulldogs. There were plenty of Georgia high-school stars on Tennessee's 1998 football team, but those three signified a shift in recruiting for the Vols, who didn't have the luxury to rely on in-state talent like Florida and Georgia. Signing Grant, Lewis, and Coleman in 1997 made a monstrous statement in recruiting circles.

"A huge one," Grant said with a laugh. "It just spoke volumes of (Tennessee's) recruiting back then because they got me, which was one of the number-one defensive backs in the country at the time. Jamal was a top-five running back, was an All-American. Cosey Coleman was a top three offensive lineman in the country. He was an All-American, also."

Cosey Coleman

The trio were stars for the Vols. Grant became a consensus first-team All-American. Coleman was named second-team All-American. Lewis was injured often during his career at Tennessee, but was clearly an elite back. He later went on to become only the eighth running back in NFL history to rush for over 2,000 yards in a season.

How close was Grant to actually going to Georgia? Very. Had he done that it would have sent repercussions throughout the SEC that would have undermined the Vols in the 1998 Florida game long before tickets were printed.

"Georgia was so hard on me that at one point I was about to commit to Georgia," Grant said.

Grant didn't have to worry about fitting in at Tennessee. He was immediately embraced by his fellow safety, Fred White, shortly after arriving on campus.

"It was awesome," Grant said. "Two Georgia boys. He was serving as a big brother when I first came in. From day one, the synergy was there. They used to call us 'Thunder and Lightning.' He brought the boom and I was going to roam through the sky. It was awesome."

When Grant, Coleman, and Lewis signed with Tennessee out of the Peach State, they had one specific goal in mind—to beat the Gators.

"That was our mentality every time we faced Florida," Grant said. "In our mind, that was always our goal."

That recruiting coup didn't just happen. Led by Fulmer, who was considered one of the top recruiters in the nation, the Vols had to start from the ground floor when they recruited elite players out of Georgia, especially Grant.

"I'm going to be honest. I didn't know anything about Tennessee before they started recruiting me, before Coach Fulmer came and sat inside my mom's living room. He was the only coach that did that. Let me make that part clear. We were still staying in the lower-income area, in the projects."

"He actually came and sat in the living room and had a face-to-face conversation with my mother. That stood out to me, gave my mom that trust that I was going to be taken care of.

"That little piece of 'we need you,' I knew that I would have an opportunity to play early at Tennessee."

Grant was the back end of a stellar group of defensive backs. White was the other safety. Dwayne Goodrich and Steve Johnson were the starting cornerbacks. The Vols were really, really good in the secondary and they knew it. If there was any doubt about that fact, Grant's interception hammered it home. That confidence grew throughout the season and was at its peak before the national championship game against Florida State. In fact, the Seminoles weren't held in nearly as high regard as Florida to those in Tennessee's locker room.

"I didn't respect Florida State like that," Grant said. "I was looking at Florida State like, you've got all this hype for no reason."

In other words, the Seminoles were good, but they weren't the Gators that the Vols had vanquished five months earlier. Did Florida State's two-time All-American receiver Peter Warrick scare Tennessee?

"We knew they were good, but I didn't look at them like Florida," Grant said. "I was upset every time they were talking about Peter Warrick. I took that personal, so personal."

Goodrich took it personally, too, when the pregame hype around Warrick was so prevalent. In fact, Goodrich demanded to play Warrick one-on-one throughout the national championship game in the Fiesta Bowl. That wasn't Tennessee's style, but it was against Florida State. Instead of staying on one side of the field, Goodrich tracked Warrick like a keen hunter. Why? The Vols had confidence, especially in the secondary. Where did that come from? That's a recurring theme.

Al Wilson was always on his teammates—and not in a nice way. Whatever the method, it worked. Players just responded to Wilson despite the aggressive attitude and rather coarse language he leaned on. Grant certainly knew what it was like to get called out by Wilson. It happened in the Mississippi State game in 1998. Grant may have been cemented as one of the top safeties in college football, but he wasn't above Wilson's wrath even in the 1998 SEC Championship Game.

"He cursed me out," Grant said of Wilson. "This is on the field. He curse me out so bad, but he cursed me out from a motivation standpoint. I don't want to repeat all the things he said, but it was him going directly at me. Why he chose to go directly at me? I guess he felt like I'm going to need Deon on this play. That's the play when I went up and blocked the field goal. He happened to catch the field goal and ran it back. You couldn't even draw that up that it ended up happening like that."

Tennessee won the game 24-14, but they trailed 14-10 in the fourth quarter. A loss against the Bulldogs would have been one of the most devastating losses in Tennessee football history. That meant Wilson's speech essentially saved the season by pushing Grant to make another essential play.

"It definitely brought something out of me that I was able to go up and block the field goal and it just so happened that he was the one that was able to run that back," Grant said.

Was that confidence always there among the Georgia prospects? Perhaps. However, that one interception against Florida was proof that the Vols could play free and aggressive. There was no reason to worry about the previous games against the Gators.

"I felt comfortable going up with one hand, but I didn't draw it up like that," Grant said. "I was very surprised that I came down with it. I thought I was going to break the pass up, but when I got my hand on it and felt like I could bring it in, I was definitely surprised and excited when I got to the sideline."

The following moments were some of the most special in Tennessee football history. The Vols beat Florida 20-17. Legendary broadcaster John Ward famously yelled, "Pandemonium Reigns!!!" as the fans charged the field. That didn't happen often. Tennessee was expected to win most of their home games. In fact, it would take 24 years for the Vols to give fans ample reason to charge the field. That occurred in a 52-49 win against Alabama in 2022 under second-year coach Josh Heupel, who strangely enough has drawn comparisons to Spurrier. However, there is one big difference between Spurrier and Heupel: Spurrier liked to talk—a lot.

Spurrier, who was a high-school star at Science Hill High School in Johnson City, Tennessee, liked to poke fun at the Vols while he was at Florida. He would drop quips often, such as you can't spell Citrus Bowl without a "U" and a "T," and Peyton Manning could aspire to become a three-time Citrus Bowl MVP. Ouch. That must have stung considering there was such a massive fall off from playing for a national championship to middling in the meaningless Citrus Bowl, which was essentially the home to the second-place team in the SEC East at the time. However, Spurrier had nothing to say after the 1998 game and the quips stopped after the Vols won the national championship in 1998.

There isn't one play that determines a national championship, but if one play had to be chosen, it was certainly the Grant interception against Florida. One play in September led to a win against an archrival. One play in September showcased Tennessee's confidence and talent.

Tennessee beat Florida State 23-16 in the national championship game. However, that would have never happened had Grant not hauled in that interception. It had been 47 years since Tennessee had won a national title. That was all erased with a new attitude, a new influx of talent, and that one interception. Simply put, that one play led to pandemonium and it reigned throughout the Vols on their way to a college football championship.

CHAPTER 9

The Fumble

The game was essentially over, as were Tennessee's national championship hopes. Oh well, it was a great run.

The Vols won eight consecutive games to start the 1998 season before they hosted Arkansas. They'd risen to No. 1. A UT win would mean the Vols' national title hopes would stay alive. An Arkansas loss would end the Vols' dreams for a title but keep hope alive for the Razorbacks, who were surprisingly also in the national title hunt. That's where things were headed as Arkansas' quarterback Clint Stoerner lined up under center on second down with just 1:47 left on the clock. Arkansas needed twelve yards for the first down, but that wasn't even necessary.

If Arkansas could just run the clock and punt the ball deep, they'd likely upset the top-ranked Vols in Neyland Stadium. As UT's defense tried to hold on, quarterback Tee Martin and UT Offensive Coordinator David Cutcliffe were devising a drive in which they'd have very little time left—if they got the ball back at all. Turns out, that conversation was all for naught thanks to Billy Ratliff.

"I'm going to try to jump the snap, get off the ball as quick as possible, and I'm going to put my hand straight on his chest and run him through the goalpost," Ratliff said recently when asked what he remembered about the play that would most define UT's national championship season. "Sure enough, it happened. I pushed Brandon back. He was on his heels and I was like, 'I'm not going to stop pushing.'"

Brandon was Brandon Burlsworth, an All-American offensive guard who began his career at Arkansas as a walk-on and was known for his thick, black glasses. Until that point in the game, he had his way with the Vols, including Ratliff.

Tennessee offensive coordinator Randy Sanders with QB Tee Martin

"He whipped my butt that whole game," Ratliff said.

Except for one play.

Ratliff's explosive push into the backfield caused Burlsworth to step on Stoerner's foot. Stoerner tried to balance himself with right hand. There was only one problem. That hand was holding the football. Stoerner lost his grip as he seemingly laid the ball on the ground.

Arkansas QB Clint Stoerner fumbles against Tennessee

"All of the sudden I looked down and I see the ball on the ground," Ratliff said. "I promise you that ball seemed like it was there for 5 or 6 seconds."

Ratliff pounced on the ball. Suddenly, the Vols had the ball in Arkansas territory with time to mount a more conventional drive. The play was unpredictable, right? Not exactly.

Anyone within earshot of Ratliff just moments before heard him call his shot. UT linebacker Al Wilson witnessed his teammate's proclamation to Martin on the sideline.

"Billy Ratliff was right next to me," Wilson said. "Tee came off the field and Billy told him, 'Hey man, don't put your helmet away. We're going to get the ball back.'"

It was the offense's turn after Ratliff proved prophetic. UT took over at the Hogs' 43-yard line with just 1:43 left. All Martin had to do was hand the ball off to running back Travis Henry. Cutcliffe called on Henry five consecutive times. The final carry was a one-yard touchdown run with 28 seconds left and an eventual 28-24 win.

It was an interesting set of play calls for Cutcliffe, who is widely considered a quarterback and passing game guru. Surely, UT head coach Phillip Fulmer called the shots, given his background. Fulmer was a former offensive lineman who loved running the football. One of Fulmer's favorite phrases was "Pound the Rock," as in run the football until the other team breaks. Cutcliffe decided to do just that.

"That defined the Tennessee offense that year," Cutcliffe said. "Phillip was saying, 'We've got to throw it. We've got to throw it.' I said, 'No, we're going to run it every down' and we ran the football right down their throat."

Said Fulmer, "Anybody that loves football would love that. You take the ball and drive it and run almost the same play, sometimes right, sometimes left, but basically the same play and run it down their throat and win the game and don't leave hardly any time on the clock. I love that, whether it's as (a former) lineman or just a person that likes sports. You like to see those kinds of things happen in sports. It was a legendary drive for sure."

One of the most unusual aspects of the Arkansas fumble is that Ratliff shouldn't have been in the game at all. Ratliff replaced fellow defensive lineman Jeff Coleman, who was suffering from cramps on the sideline when Ratliff made history.

"I tell people all the time that if I was still in the game when that happened, we probably would have lost because I just didn't have it in the tank right then," Coleman said. "Billy was great. He had fresh legs and blew up the play."

Ratliff and Coleman were suite mates, so they knew each other well off the field. Coleman had seen the pain Ratliff had been through. During his UT career, Ratliff suffered a severe neck injury, two torn knee ligaments, and serious shin splints. Yet Ratliff kept fighting through his injuries to help his teammates.

"If Billy Ratliff is still out here playing, whatever injury I have, it can't be that bad," Coleman said. "He inspires people. He keeps getting knocked down and coming back."

Considering the medical issues, an NFL career wasn't likely in the works. Ratliff continued playing football for the love of the game. When relatively healthy, Ratliff showed he had elite talent. Coleman recalled seeing Ratliff, who was over 300 pounds, dunk a basketball with a torn anterior cruciate ligament.

"He was freak athlete. He definitely was," Coleman said. "That's one of those that I would have loved to have seen his career if he had not been injured. He was already something special, but it would have been something else had he not gone through the injuries he did."

The Arkansas win did more than preserve the Vols' perfect record. It made them believe they could win a title, and it instilled fear of the possibility of coming up short.

"After the Arkansas game, we knew that was our moment," former UT cornerback Dwayne Goodrich said.

Said Martin, "It was really good for us as a team to win in the fashion we won. I really felt like that game built character in our team because for the first time, we felt the feeling of defeat and that was a feeling we didn't want to have anymore."

That wouldn't be the case. The Vols finished the regular season by blasting Kentucky 59-21 and Vanderbilt 41-0. There was no overlooking those two foes like the Vols almost did against Arkansas.

CHAPTER 10

Losing a Leader

Tennessee Offensive Coordinator David Cutcliffe had made countless play calls, chosen hundreds of starting lineups, and helped guide six seasons worth of game plans. None of those compared to what he was facing late in 1998.

"That may be the most difficult decision I've ever made in my whole life," the former Tennessee offensive coordinator said while reminiscing about the Vols' championship season.

Cutcliffe was referring to his decision to leave the Vols just a month before the national championship game. As the man in charge of Tennessee's offense, Cutcliffe led the Vols to an SEC Championship and a 12-0 season in 1998, but Ole Miss came calling and the Rebels had a coaching vacancy to fill.

Cutcliffe interviewed for the Rebels' head coaching position before the 1998 SEC Championship Game. He was expected to land the Ole Miss job—his first head coaching position—after being an assistant at UT since 1982. However, there was one problem. Ole Miss wanted Cutcliffe now. The Rebels were set to play Texas Tech in the Independence Bowl and they didn't have a coaching staff after Tommy Tuberville had left Ole Miss for Auburn.

Cutcliffe decided he had to leave the Vols immediately and join his new team in Oxford. Before he left, he had to tell the Vols.

"I cried in front of that team," Cutcliffe said. "I cried at home, literally cried. I grieved."

The Vols were fortunate that they had nearly a month to formulate a plan to play Florida State in the Fiesta Bowl. They were also fortunate that

Randy Sanders

they had a capable back-up ready to step in. The Vols turned to assistant coach Randy Sanders to lead the offense. Fulmer could have handled the task, but he had plenty to do.

"That was the best answer," Fulmer said. "It was either me or him. We kind of worked together to do it and he called every play. It all worked out great."

Sanders, who played quarterback at UT from 1984-88 and joined the staff a year later, was ready for the daunting task that Fulmer had chosen for him.

"I was hoping what I had done in the previous ten years coaching had given him reason to think I could do it, but it was still up to him and it was his decision. ... I'm just thankful he gave me the opportunity to do it and I'm glad it worked out like it did," Sanders said.

Fulmer understood the loss of Cutcliffe was significant, but he wouldn't let his team wallow in it.

"We weren't going to let it be a distraction," Fulmer said. "We talked about it briefly. David felt like for him that he needed to be with his team there. Certainly we hated it because he wasn't going to get to be a part (of the national title game and) it could leave us short, but it didn't.

"You have to give great credit to Randy Sanders and the offensive staff. We all chipped in and nothing changed. In some ways it might have been a little better for us because it was a different style than what Florida State might have been working on. It was a different person calling the plays, but if I'd have my druthers and you could get him (Cutcliffe) to totally commit to him being here, I'd probably druther he stayed."

Sanders understood the importance of a potential national title because he knew UT so well. He was well aware that the Vols hadn't won a national title since 1951. Sanders began as a quarterbacks coach, then coached receivers before moving to running backs and becoming UT's recruiting coordinator from 1993-1998. However, his new Fiesta Bowl assignment was something far different.

Phillip Fulmer

The Fiesta Bowl was the first time Sanders would be an offensive coordinator. It was the first time he would handle all of the play calling. It was the first time he was in charge.

"It was definitely the first time I had ever called a complete game and it was the first time I had ever been primarily responsible for the game plan to get to that point," Sanders said. "I don't remember it being that nerve-wracking. I remember feeling the awesome responsibility to fulfill my role for that football team."

Sanders recalls the Fiesta Bowl bowl trip well, but doesn't recall seeing much of his family during the pregame events.

"Yeah, that was the week we didn't see Daddy the whole time," Sanders recalls his wife saying. "I don't remember going to one bowl function that week. I don't remember getting back to my hotel in daylight that whole week. I would wake up before daylight, go to the film room, go to what we had set up as our offensive staff room, work, go to practice, come back, work, and then when it came time to go to bed I would just go to bed. I ate almost all of my meals in that (work) room."

Sanders moved from the sideline to the press box for the Fiesta Bowl. Sitting in that seat with a national title on the line wasn't daunting to Sanders; it was exhilarating.

"It was fun," he said. "It was exciting. It was a little bit of a 'wow' moment."

At the same time Sanders was thinking 'wow,' Cutcliffe was in another place. Now Ole Miss' head coach, Cutcliffe sat in a rental home watching the game he had worked his entire career to be a part of. Cutcliffe's family was still back in Knoxville. Alone, he only had his thoughts to keep him company as the Vols won their first national championship by beating the Seminoles 23-16.

"Man, I cried and I cried with joy," Cutcliffe said. "I felt like I was having an out-of-body experience watching that team play. When it was all said and done, I've never felt more joy or pride in anything."

Cutcliffe began calling his former fellow coaches as soon as the game was over. The first person he got on the phone was his replacement. After speaking to Sanders, the phone was passed around the locker room so Cutcliffe could be a part of the celebration.

"I stayed up all night," Cutcliffe said. "There was no way I was going to bed. I just kept thinking of the season, a perfect season, and what a national championship meant to the Tennessee fans and people that had gone through the '90s and (were) so close over and over again.

"To culminate my time there with a team winning a national championship, I don't know if I slept the next night. It was an amazing feeling."

Cutcliffe could have been there in person. Fulmer invited Cutcliffe to come to Tempe, Arizona, after Ole Miss' Independence Bowl. Cutcliffe declined.

Tennessee's 1998 National Championship Ring

"I just felt like it was going to disrupt," he said. "It was very hard telling him I don't need to do that."

Cutcliffe has more than just rental-home memories of UT winning a national title. He has a memento that symbolizes what he meant to the Vols, a national championship ring.

"I earned that," Cutcliffe said. "I don't have any qualms. I display that very proudly in my house."

CHAPTER 11

Managing Men

As with any elite team, Tennessee's coaches pressed all the right buttons on multiple occasions through the spring, summer, and fall. There was a point during preseason camp in 1998 when the Vols' offensive players decided they'd had enough of being pushed around. They might not have been an elite offensive unit with all the sizzle and fireworks that are so common today, but they knew they were tough and were ready to prove it. They just needed to be challenged.

The challenge came from Tennessee's coaches, led by head coach Phillip Fulmer, who didn't like the fact that camp had gotten so chippy and the offense was getting the short end of the altercations more times than not. So he challenged his offense before one of the final full-contact practices of fall camp.

"He said 'It's time to get tough and let's whoop somebody's ass in practice. You're not going to bully us no more. We're going to be the bullies in the barnyard,'" Riley recalled Fulmer saying about Tennessee's defense. "I got that. I understood that 100 percent."

Indeed. During a running play, Riley laid out Al Wilson from his blindside. The two exchanged verbal barbs, then fisticuffs, then it was on.

"It was not a melee. It was an all-out freaking brawl," Riley said. "We all were in it. It was one of my favorite memories of all time because that's, I swear, where we got to be a good football club."

Being a former offensive lineman and offensive line coach, Fulmer didn't need to be told that his offense was getting beat—and beaten badly—in preseason camp with the season pressing down upon them.

"Those were grown men on defense, but those were grown men on offense, too," Fulmer said. "It took them a while to make up their mind they weren't going to get bullied."

There are fights in football practice that can be helpful, harmful, or have no impact at all. As for the *Great Practice Fight of 1998*, it had an immediate impact.

Suddenly, Tennessee's defense had a little more respect for its offensive counterparts. However, the key was that no one held a grudge off the practice field, not even in the locker room after the infamous practice. The Vols were tough and aggressive while also closely bonded. That meant they were always respectful of one another even in the most intense moments. A physical practice with a fierce brawl could be followed up with a cookout with everyone invited just a day later. Fights never went past the football field. No foes. Just brothers.

Fulmer knew that kinship was there and used it to push his team to the edge of chaos in practice. He also proved that he knew how to prepare a team for their biggest game, which meant finishing the deal and winning the national championship in the Fiesta Bowl against Florida State.

Fulmer has long said that he patterned his coaching style after Tom Osborne, the Nebraska head coach who had led the Cornhuskers to that dominating win over the Vols in the Orange Bowl before the 1998 season. Osborne didn't allow his players to talk any trash during the pregame festivities leading up to the game. Fulmer did the same as the Vols were preparing for Florida State a year later. He never wanted his team to talk trash through the media or during bowl festivities, but he made doubly sure to place a gag order on his team before the Fiesta Bowl in January of 1999. That made sense, considering the game would determine the first Bowl Championship Series National Championship. No team would want to be undone by a wayward quote that jilted their upcoming foe.

"I always liked being the underdog or being perceived as the underdog," said Fulmer, who admitted to playing the "disrespect card" often during his tenure and did so before the Fiesta Bowl.

Then, the gag order was lifted (at least the players thought so) just before the final bowl game festivity that was held in Tempe at a local amusement park. The Vols let loose on the Seminoles, who were widely considered significant favorites to beat Tennessee, with a verbal tirade predicting what was going to happen in the game. Florida State's players were taken aback. This wasn't the meek team that Tennessee had seemed to be all week. The Vols were a team that was mad, felt disrespected all season long, and came ready to play.

Tennessee WR Peerless Price reels in a 79-yard TD pass

Fulmer was well known for poking and prodding his players in any way possible, oftentimes through the media in order to elicit a reaction that could inspire a team deep in the middle of preseason camp. However, it was a joke that set up the Vols for their thirty minutes of football, which turned out to be a second half in which they would hold the Seminoles to just seven meaningless points. While no one can quite recall the joke exactly, every player remembered the reaction, a chuckle then a let-it-all-loose mentality in the second half that would secure the Vols' place in history. Fulmer wasn't one to tell jokes at halftime. When he did, it had an impact.

"I know I did not want them to be puckered up," he said.

It wasn't the only motivational tool Fulmer used that season. He also used a walking stick that would go to the position group that graded out

Phillip Fulmer

the highest each week. Even Fulmer admitted that he thought it was a bit silly at first, but the players eventually took pride in having the stick in their individual position meetings each week.

"Moses led his people to the promised land," Fulmer recalled telling his team early in the preseason, "and I'm telling you right now that if you keep working like you guys are, I'm going to lead you to the promised land. The stick was the first thing on the bus, first thing off the airplane and the first thing on the sideline."

Be it a stick, a halftime joke, or a preseason fight, Tennessee's football team did indeed make it to the promised land, which happened to be in Arizona that year. When the game and season had played out, the Vols were undefeated and there was no argument who deserved the national title.

Tennessee had beaten Florida State 23-16, finished the season with a 13-0 record as the only unbeaten Division I team in the country. The

Phillp Fulmer

Vols were the first BCS National Champion and secured Tennessee's first football championship in 47 years.

Talent, deft coaching, and some fortunate turns of events throughout the season helped make a championship possible. However, there would have been no banners hung had it not been for the bond that Tennessee's players built from the first moments they walked on campus, bonds that carried them through the season and are still strong to this day.

The Vols had done what they came to do. Won it all.

It was indeed time to celebrate.

CHAPTER 12

What I Learned

Here are the thirteen most significant things that I learned about the 1998 Vols:

1. Tennessee's players were tattletales (in a good way)

I never would have imagined that UT's football players had so much power and weren't afraid to wield it. If a player on the 1998 team wasn't working hard enough in practice or off-season workouts, the team leaders would tell their coaches those players shouldn't play. And the coaches listened.

2. The Vols held full practices during what were supposed to be summer workouts

Former UT quarterback Peyton Manning was known for his dedication to off-season workouts and coercing teammates to participate. However, with Manning and other leaders from the 1997 team gone, the Vols upped the intensity with full workouts without pads or coaches all summer. According to several Vols, that made preseason camp easy.

3. Al Wilson became a leader during the 1997 SEC Championship Game

Wilson had never won a significant championship when the Vols trailed Auburn at halftime in the 1997 SEC Championship Game. The fiery middle linebacker wasn't going to let that one slide by. Wilson challenged

Manning and defensive end Leonard Little that night and, subsequently, assumed the leadership role that would define him for the 1998 season.

David Cutcliffe

4. David Cutcliffe was very concerned about UT's offense before the season

Cutcliffe, UT's offensive coordinator, never said he was worried about UT's offense in public before spring practice or again before fall camp, but he was. Cutcliffe knew a Manning-like approach wouldn't work, so he had to adapt. He eventually decided to field a power running football team. It worked. Tennessee actually increased its scoring average to 33.2 from 32.9 from 1997, just in a very different way.

5. Phillip Fulmer thought the Georgia game was a key turning point

I would have thought the Florida game was the early season game in which the Vols began to believe. However, Fulmer thought the Georgia game as significant or even more so. The Vols hammered the Bulldogs 22-3 in Athens to get to 5-0. In retrospect, Fulmer's thoughts on the game makes sense. UT won a rival game on the road just one week after losing their offensive focal point, tailback Jamal Lewis, to a knee injury for the remainder of the season.[]

Phillip Fulmer

6. Al Wilson wasn't afraid to fight teammates on national television

There is intensity. Then there is Wilson intensity. Wilson challenged safety Fred White to a fight if he ever slowed up on a play after White had done so early in the season. White never did that again. That intensity permeated through UT's defense in 1998.

Al Wilson

7. The Arkansas fumble should have never happened

Admittedly, defensive tackle Jeff Coleman said the infamous fumble against Arkansas would have never taken place had he been in the game because he was gassed. That opened the door for Billy Ratliff to take Coleman's place. The rest is history.

Razorback QB Clint Stoerner fumbling in the f nal minutes of UT-Arkansas game

8. The Arkansas game bonded the Vols immensely

Tasting potential defeat and rising from the ashes changed the Vols' mindset in the Arkansas game. They hoped and thought they could be a national championship team before beating the Razorbacks in dramatic fashion. The Vols absolutely knew they would be champions after escaping with a victory against the Hogs.

9. The Vols knew Cutcliffe would be hired by Ole Miss before the SEC Championship Game

Coaches like to say distractions don't affect them, but that's not really true. UT's offense started slowly against Mississippi State in the SEC Championship Game perhaps because of Cutcliffe's pending departure, which was almost common knowledge to the team. Still, the Vols persevered and beat Mississippi State 24-14 to win their second consecutive SEC title and a chance to play for a national championship.

10. Randy Sanders wasn't sure he'd be called on to replace Cutcliffe for the Fiesta Bowl

This seemed like a no-brainer at the time, but Fulmer had a decision to make. He could have chosen someone else to take Cutcliffe's place, or Fulmer could have assumed game-plan and play-calling duties himself, but he trusted Sanders. That turned out to be a great call.

Randy Sanders

11. Dwayne Goodrich didn't speak to any teammates during his jail stay

I expected Goodrich, UT's standout defensive back, to tell me that his teammates helped him get through his eight-year jail sentence. That wasn't the case. Goodrich withdrew from his teammates because he was ashamed of his actions. The Vols welcomed Goodrich back with open arms when he was released.

Dwayne Goodrich

12. Ratliff still thinks about Brandon Burlsworth every day

Billy Ratliff hasn't forgotten about the player, offensive lineman Brandon Burlsworth, who mostly dominated the game before the most memorable fumble in Tennessee football history. Ratliff said his own son reminds him of the fragility of life. That further reminds Ratliff of Burlsworth, who was Arkansas' All-American offensive guard. According to several former players, Burlsworth beat up on UT's defensive line in the Arkansas game. Ratliff didn't hold a grudge and has always kept Burlsworth and his family in his heart. Burlsworth died in a car wreck in 1999, eleven days after being drafted.

Brandon Burlsworth

13. Wilson's son is cured and doing well

Wilson's son was diagnosed with brain cancer when he was fifteen years old. That didn't stop the young man. Carrington Wilson graduated from Triveca University where he was still a baseball player. He is currently in medical school.

Carrington Wilson

CHAPTER 13

Where are they now

FB: Shawn Bryson

1998: Bryson, according to former UT head coach Phillip Fulmer, embodied the selflessness of the Vols in 1998. Bryson had the ability to play tailback but with a crowded backfield. He assumed the role of a consistent blocker and explosive runner at fullback.

After: Bryson immersed himself in coaching. He's the head coach at Rabun Gap-Nacoochee School in North Carolina. He was recently selected to the National Football League Bill Walsh Diversity Fellowship Coaching Program.

LT: Chad Clifton

1998: Clifton was in charge of protecting Martin's blindside on passing plays and helping the Vols' dominant running game.

After: Clifton went from protecting Martin in college to protecting Brett Favre in the NFL. After being selected in the second round of the 2000 NFL Draft, Clifton was chosen to play in two Pro Bowls and won a Super Bowl with the Green Bay Packers. Clifton was the victim of a violent hit by former NFL defensive lineman Warren Sapp that caused a severe pelvic injury. Clifton eventually returned and the NFL expanded the "unnecessary roughness" rule to include hits like Sapp's.

RG: Cosey Coleman

1998: Coleman was probably the most physically gifted of UT's 1998 offensive linemen. He was also a key signee for the Vols. He was part of an incredible trio of Atlanta-area recruits the Vols signed in 1997, along with running back Jamal Lewis and safety Deon Grant. Coleman was named first-team All-SEC and second-team All-American.

After: Coleman was selected in the second round of the 2000 NFL Draft by the Tampa Bay Buccaneers. He would play five seasons for the Bucs and two for the Cleveland Browns to finish his career.

S: Deon Grant

1998: No one can forget the interception Grant made against Florida. He was a consistent force in the Vols' secondary in 1998 and 1999 before leaving Tennessee early to enter the NFL Draft. Grant was named a consensus All-American while at Tennessee.

After: Grant played eleven seasons in the NFL and won Super Bowl XLVI with the New York Giants. Grant currently runs his GRANT foundation and works for the Players Association (NFLPA) to help them make the transition from football to retirement. He's also a part owner of a professional basketball team in Australia, some restaurants, a nightclub, and a water-ice company. He invested in a marijuana business in San Francisco and still trains players for college and professional football.

K: Jeff Hall

1998: Hall was the clutch kicker that Tennessee needed with a football team that was destined to play close games due to their dependency on running the football and playing tough defense. His winning kick against Florida is one of the most memorable kicks in Tennessee football history.

After: Hall is a financial planner in Knoxville.

LG: Mercedes Hamilton

1998: Hamilton was the quiet mauler of UT's 1998 offensive line. Like his fellow linemen, he was key in opening running holes for UT's talented corps of running backs.

After: Hamilton is currently a Machine Tech at Bridgestone in Atlanta, according to his Linkedin account. Hamilton is also a high-school football coach.

RB: Travis Henry

1998: Henry stepped in for Lewis and helped the Vols stay dominant in the running game. Henry's hard, physical style wasn't quite as explosive as Lewis but it punished defenses. The Vols barely missed a beat with Henry in the lineup.

After: Henry rushed for 6,086 yards for the Buffalo Bills, Tennessee Titans, and Denver Broncos after being selected in the 2001 NFL Draft. After his career, he moved back to Florida before moving back to Nashville.

RB: Jamal Lewis

1998: Lewis was the focal point of UT's offense until he went down with a knee injury in the Auburn game that would end his season.

After: After returning from his knee injury, Lewis showed his freakish athletic ability was still intact during the 1999 season and in workouts for the NFL. He was picked fifth overall in the 1999 NFL Draft. Lewis ran for 10,607 yards during his NFL career, including 2,066 yards in 2003. He is currently the president of Southeast Exhibits and Metro Retail Solutions.

QB: Tee Martin

1998: Martin stepped into former UT quarterback Peyton Manning's position and handled it quite well. With a strong arm and the ability to run the football, Martin turned in key plays that would help the Vols to their perfect record.

After: Martin was considered for at least two coaching positions in which he could have returned to UT, but the two parties couldn't come to an agreement. Martin is currently a quarterbacks coach for the Baltimore Ravens.

WR: Peerless Price

Peerless Price with daughter Caeden

1998: Price was the deep threat that the Vols needed to keep defenses honest in 1998. His chemistry with Martin was sublime on deep-passing routes.

After: Price played nine season in the NFL for the Buffalo Bills, Dallas Cowboys, and Atlanta Falcons. He currently coaches his daughter's AAU basketball team.

RT: Jarvis Reado

1998: Reado would have been the starting left tackle on most other teams had the Vols not had Clifton. Instead, Reado manned the right side of UT's offensive line.

After: Reado is a trustee in Knox County.

C: Spencer Riley

1998: In addition to handling the middle of UT's offensive line, Riley was always the funny member of the offense and always good for a quote for assembled reporters. Riley was the overachiever of the group but he handled that role well.

After: Riley climbed his way up the high school coaching ladder before he was named the head coach of his alma mater, Jefferson County High School, in 2016 and is currently still there.

LB: Al Wilson

1998: The clear leader of the team, Wilson was a team captain on the 1998 SEC Championship team. Wilson was named a consensus first-team All-American following the '98 season. He was then selected in the first round of the 1999 NFL Draft, played eight seasons in the NFL, was selected to five Pro Bowls and named All-Pro twice. Wilson retired following the 2006 season, partly due to an injured back.

After: Wilson currently lives in Atlanta. Retired from football, Wilson is a part of a handful of businesses. His son, Carrington, is currently in medical school.

WR: Cedrick Wilson

1998: Wilson was an underrated receiver after he moved from quarterback, where he played in high school. Overlooking Wilson was understandable, considering he was playing next to Peerless Price, who would go on to star in the NFL. Wilson also followed former UT standouts Marcus Nash and Joey Kent. However, Wilson was a master of getting in and out of his breaks at full speed.

After: After seven years in the NFL, Wilson became a high-school coach and has pursued business in the restaurant field.

S: Fred White

1998: White was asked to be selfless early in his career. After being recruited as a cornerback, White was asked to move to safety where he flourished as one of the hardest hitting safeties in SEC history.

After: White is still very involved with all of his teammates and organizes various events in which they can reunite. After a career in the NFL and XFL, White owns his own Allstate insurance agency.

NATIONAL AND SOUTHEASTERN CONFERENCE CHAMPIONS

1998 University of Tennessee Volunteers

Front Row (L-R): Henderson, White, Miles, Plemons, Hall, Veazey, Copeland, Grant, Mathews, Marsh, B. Scott, Loudermilk, B. Graham, Gaines, Golden, Brown, C. Wilson. **Second Row:** Sewell, Reagan, T. Martin, Griffin, Seabrooks, Wortman, Henry, Horne, Crosby, Terry, Goodrich, Bryson, Stephens, Ewart, L. Scott, A. Wilson. **Third Row:** Stevenson, Allen, Lott, Lewis, Edmonds, St. Johnson, Sh. Johnson, Fitzgerald, Price, Alexander, Hurst, Frogg, James, Ratliff, Ramseur, Westmoreland, Leaverton, Kemp. **Fourth Row:** Bartholomew, Thompson, Biggers, Blankenship, Atherton, Dougharty, Whiteside, Gregory, C. Coleman, Champion, Robinson, Green, Jackson, Colston, Walker, Granzow, Goodin. **Fifth Row:** Emert, Richardson, Whiteside, Roe, T. Stallworth, Clifton, Riley, Massa, Bostic, R. Coleman, Reado, Campbell, Ofenheusle, Gooden, Hamilton, Satterfield, Verive, Tucker, Hodges. **Sixth Row:** Ridley, Parker, Kendrick, Houston, Diogu, T. Graham, N. Johnson, D. Stallworth, Jones, Carr, D. Martin, Kent, Moore, Smith, Starks, Overstreet, Hand, J. Coleman, Ellis, Butler. **Seventh Row:** Weary, Finlayson, Jameson, Roper, Brooks, Barry, Sanders, Cutcliffe, Fulmer, Holloway, Chavis, Blackburn, Ramsey, Washington, Bradley, Reid, Peebles, Lloyd.

Neyland Stadium in 1998

About Dave Hooker

Dave Hooker has covered Tennessee football for over 25 years. The award-winning writer/talk show host has worked for various media outlets including ESPN and the flagship station of the Vol Network, and he has appeared on multiple national platforms as a college football analyst. A Powell High School alumnus, Dave graduated from the University of Tennessee in 1998, which happened to be a pretty good year for the Vols. He has two children and resides in East Tennessee.

Fresh Ink Group

Independent Multi-media Publisher

Fresh Ink Group / Push Pull Press

Voice of Indie / GeezWriter

Hardcovers

Softcovers

All Ebook Formats

Audiobooks

Podcasts

Worldwide Distribution

Indie Author Services

Book Development, Editing, Proofing

Graphic/Cover Design

Video/Trailer Production

Website Creation

Social Media Marketing

Writing Contests

Writers' Blogs

Authors

Editors

Artists

Experts

Professionals

FreshInkGroup.com

info@FreshInkGroup.com

Twitter: @FreshInkGroup

Facebook.com/FreshInkGroup

LinkedIn: Fresh Ink Group

Printed in the USA
CPSIA information can be obtained
at www.ICGtesting.com
LVHW070021081123
763115LV00038B/1258/J

9 781958 922477